BITCOIN PRIMER

BY

Dennis Roeder

Disclaimer:

The information presented in this book is intended for general informational and educational purposes only. The authors and publishers do not provide financial, investment, or legal advice. The content is not intended as professional guidance for cryptocurrency usage. Each individual's situation is unique, and one should always conduct thorough research and due diligence before making decisions regarding cryptocurrency investments or usage.

The authors make no representations or warranties of any kind, express or implied, about the completeness or accuracy of the contents of this book. The information provided may contain errors or omissions. The authors and publishers disclaim any liability for any loss or damage incurred as a consequence of the use and application of the contents of this book.

Investment in cryptocurrency entails risk of financial loss. Historical performance is no guarantee of future returns. Nothing in this book shall be construed as a solicitation to invest in any program, cryptocurrency, token, protocol, or project. Those interested should only invest based on their own determination of the merits and risks involved after consulting with financial and legal professionals as appropriate.

Past performance does not guarantee future results. Any investment or usage decisions made by readers upon relying on the book shall be at their own accountability and discretion. The authors and publishers shall have no liability for any consequences arising from decisions or actions taken by any reader of this book.

Table of Contents

Introduction

Welcome to the Bitcoin Primer, your gateway to the exciting world of cryptocurrencies and to the Digital Revolution which is reshaping the way we think about money. Whether you are a curious newbie looking to unravel the mysteries of Bitcoin or an experienced crypto enthusiast looking to increase your understanding, this book is your compass through the uncharted waters it takes the decentralized economy.

In an ever-evolving digital economy, Bitcoin stands as a symbol of innovation and decentralization, pushing the boundaries of what is possible in the world of money and communication. As you embark on this journey, you will discover the fascinating story of the creation of Bitcoin, the intricacies of the underlying technology, and the practicalities of buying, storing and using currency

From the shadow of its mysterious creator to the shining promise of financial inclusion and digital transformation Bitcoin Primer explores every aspect of the cryptocurrency universe we will discuss its role as an investment, its potential to revolutionize global payments, and its significance in a world where traditional financial systems are undergoing a profound transformation

In this book you'll find clear explanations, real-world examples, and practical guidance to help you navigate the complexities of the crypto landscape. Whether you're a future investor, an aspiring miner, or just curious about the frontier of digital finance, you'll have the knowledge and insight you need to navigate this fascinating terrain.

So, whether you are eager to unlock the mysteries of Bitcoin or deepen your understanding of the crypto universe, join us as we embark on this educational journey. Let's set sail and explore the world of Cryptocurrency together.

Chapter 1:

Introduction to Bitcoin.

In the vast realm of digital finance, Bitcoin stands as a shining beacon of innovation and decentralization. It has taken the world by storm, captivating the imagination of millions and sparking a financial revolution. This chapter serves as our portal into the captivating world of Bitcoin, introducing you to the essential aspects and significance of this groundbreaking Bitcoin.

A Digital Revolution

Imagine a world where currency isn't printed by governments and regulated by central banks. Instead, picture a global currency that exists solely in the digital realm, transcending borders and defying traditional financial systems. Welcome to the world of cryptocurrencies.

Cryptocurrencies, or "crypto" for short, are digital or virtual currencies that leverage cryptography for security. They are decentralized, which means they operate independently of a central authority like a government or bank. This notion alone is revolutionary, as it challenges the conventional monetary system we've known for centuries.

Bitcoin spearheaded this digital financial revolution when it first emerged in 2008. It captured the imagination of millions who were drawn to its innovative peer-to-peer payment network and its vision of a decentralized global currency. Bitcoin showed the world that a form of money could exist entirely in the digital realm, without the need for centralized control. This was a radically new concept, and it opened up people's minds to a whole new financial system.

A Mysterious Beginning

Bitcoin made its debut in 2008 when an individual or group of individuals operating under the pseudonym Satoshi Nakamoto published a whitepaper titled "Bitcoin: A Peer-to-Peer Electronic Cash System." The true identity of Satoshi Nakamoto remains a tantalizing mystery, as this enigmatic figure chose to keep a secret identity.

Satoshi's white paper introduced the concept of a decentralized digital currency, which can be transacted directly between users without the need for banks and other intermediaries He proposed a system based on a technology called blockchain, enabling secure and transparent communication.

The release of this white paper led to the birth of bitcoin, and on January 3, 2009, the first bitcoin block called the " genesis block" was mined. This monumental event marked the beginning of an unprecedented journey that would permanently reshape the world economy. The economic revolution had begun.

The release of the blockchain

At the heart of Bitcoin's innovation is the blockchain, the sophisticated technology that underpins its operation. Blockchain is often described as a distributed ledger, which is essentially a decentralized database shared between computers. This ledger records all Bitcoin transactions chronologically and securely.

The blockchain is maintained and updated by a global network of participants known as nodes. These nodes validate and verify connections, ensuring authenticity and security. This distributed and consensus-based approach makes it virtually impossible for any one entity to operate or manage the Bitcoin network. It brings trust to an unreliable system.

The power of mining

A unique aspect of Bitcoin is the method of issuance, which involves a process called mining. Bitcoin miners are individuals or companies that use specialized hardware and software to verify and record transactions on the blockchain. In return for their efforts, miners are compensated with newly minted bitcoins.

Mining serves two crucial purposes. First, it ensures the security and integrity of the network by cryptographically verifying the validity of transactions and adding them to the blockchain. Second, it controls the supply of bitcoins entering circulation. This process follows a predetermined issuance schedule, with a diminishing block reward over time, making Bitcoin a deflationary currency.

As more miners join the network, the computational power required to mine new blocks increases, making it more challenging and competitive. This system prevents any single entity from gaining too much control over the network, maintaining its decentralized nature. Mining difficulty and competition is what keeps Bitcoin secure.

Your Digital Wallet

To interact with the world of Bitcoin, you'll need a digital wallet, which is essentially your portal to the Bitcoin. Just as you carry physical wallets to store traditional money, a digital wallet stores your Bitcoin. These wallets come in various forms, each with its unique features and security levels.

There are two main categories of digital wallets:

Hot wallets, Are connected to the internet and are convenient for everyday transactions. They are accessible through web-based platforms, mobile apps, or desktop applications. However, their internet connectivity comes with a trade-off in terms of security, as they are potentially vulnerable to online threats.

Cold wallets, on the other hand, are entirely offline and provide the highest level of security. These include hardware wallets, paper wallets, and even physical tokens. Cold wallets are used for long-term, ultra-secure storage and safeguarding significant amounts of Bitcoin.

When you create a Bitcoin wallet, you'll receive a unique address, which serves as your public key. This allows others to send bitcoins to your wallet. Additionally, your wallet generates a private key, which is essential for authorizing transactions and should be kept secret to protect your bitcoins. Protect your private keys, and your Bitcoin will be safe.

The Significance of Bitcoin

Bitcoin isn't just a new form of digital money; it's a symbol of a changing financial landscape and a challenge to the status quo. Its creation marked the start of a global movement towards decentralized currencies and blockchain technology.

The significance of Bitcoin lies in its potential to disrupt traditional financial systems and offer an alternative to centralized control and government-issued currencies. It brings the power over money back to the people. Bitcoin has the potential to bring financial services to the billions of unbanked and underbanked populations, offering a secure and accessible means of transacting and saving no matter who or where you are.

Moreover, Bitcoin is often heralded as digital gold, a potential store of value in turbulent economic times when faith in fiat currencies may falter. It provides a hedge against inflation and a means of diversifying investment portfolios. As central banks continue printing unprecedented amounts of money and governments intervene heavily in financial markets, the importance of a decentralized and deflationary asset like Bitcoin becomes increasingly apparent.

Bitcoin represents the future of money for many — a potential global currency that crosses borders and breaks down financial barriers. Still in its infancy, Bitcoin offers a glimpse into the future of the digital economy.

As we journey through the chapters of this Bitcoin Primer, we will delve into the intricacies of this amazing Currency. We'll explore the underlying technology, learn how to safely acquire and store it, understand its financial potential, and discover its real-world applications. Whether you are new to the world of cryptocurrencies or an ardent enthusiast, this book will be your guide to understanding and navigating the fascinating world of Cryptocurrency.

Chapter 2:

How Bitcoin Works.

We are going to take a laid-back stroll through the inner workings of Bitcoin. You might have heard about blockchain technology, mining, and all that jazz. Well, we're here to break it down for you in a way that even your tech-challenged aunt can understand. So, grab a comfy chair and a cup of your favorite brew, and let's dive into the intriguing world of Bitcoin.

Explaining Blockchain:

It's Like a Digital Ledger. You're in a coffee shop, sipping your latte, and chatting with your friend. You decide to lend them a few bucks, but you want it recorded somewhere, just in case. So, you both pull out your smartphones, and with a couple of taps, you update your shared digital ledger.

That digital ledger is a lot like what we call a "blockchain." It's a record-keeping system, but instead of being stored on a single computer or with a bank, it's spread across a whole network of computers. This decentralized ledger logs all Bitcoin transactions, and it's not just available for you and your friend to see. It's out there for the whole world to check

How Miners Keep the Wheels Turning

Now, let's talk about those folks we call "miners." No, they're not underground with pickaxes; they're digital prospectors. They work on verifying and recording transactions on the blockchain, ensuring everything runs smoothly in the world of Bitcoin.

Why do they do it? Well, it's not out of sheer generosity. Miners compete to solve complex mathematical puzzles, and the first one to crack it gets to add a new "block" of transactions to the blockchain. That's where the term "mining" comes from – they're mining new digital gold, a.k.a. new Bitcoins.

Here's the catch: these puzzles are designed to be super tough, and it takes a lot of computing power to solve them. As more miners join the game, the puzzles get even harder. But it's all part of the plan to keep the whole network secure. If you want to mess with the blockchain, you'd need to control more computing power than all the miners combined, and that's like saying you'll beat the entire world in a game of chess – not happening.

The Digital Gold Rush:

Bitcoin Mining,

So, what's in it for miners? Well, they're not just doing it for fun – they're rewarded with freshly minted Bitcoins and transaction fees. This process serves a couple of vital purposes. First, it verifies the legitimacy of transactions, ensuring no funny business is going on. Second, it controls the number of new Bitcoins that enter the circulation. You see, the rate of new Bitcoin creation decreases over time, making it scarcer and adding to its value. It's like mining for gold, but instead of striking the earth, you're striking code.

Your Digital Bank Account:

The Bitcoin Wallet,

Okay, now that we've got the mining basics down, let's chat about how you can get in on the action. You'll need a digital wallet, sort of like a digital bank account, but without the bank. It's where you store your hard-earned Bitcoins.

There are two main types of wallets: hot and cold. Hot wallets are like the checking account of the crypto world. They're always connected to the internet, which makes them super convenient for everyday transactions. You can access them through websites, mobile apps, or desktop programs. But here's the deal – with great convenience comes great responsibility. Hot wallets are more exposed to online threats.

Now, let's talk about the cool kids in the wallet world – cold wallets. These are the Fort Knox of crypto. They're entirely offline, making them super secure. Hardware wallets, paper wallets, and physical tokens fall into this category. They're your choice when you want to protect substantial amounts of Bitcoin, kind of like having a digital vault.

Your wallet comes with a unique address, your public key, like a digital home address. It's what people use to send you

Bitcoins. Then there's the private key, which is like the secret code to your vault. It's what you need to authorize transactions, so you better guard it like you would grandma's secret cookie recipe. Lose that, and you're locked out of your Bitcoin.

Wrapping It Up

So, why all this fuss about Bitcoin? It's not just a quirky digital experiment; it's a game-changer on several fronts.

First, Bitcoin takes the control of money out of the hands of central banks and governments. It's like a financial revolution, allowing people to have more say in how they manage their wealth. No more waiting for governments to print money; with Bitcoin, you're in the driver's seat.

Then there's the global reach of Bitcoin. It's like a lifeline for people who don't have access to traditional banks. It's a way for them to take control of their finances, even without a bank branch for miles around.

And let's not forget the "digital gold" tag. In uncertain times, people often turn to assets that hold their value. Bitcoin, with its limited supply and decentralized nature, fits that bill. It's a way to protect your wealth from inflation, economic crises, and government meddling.

As we roll through the chapters of this Bitcoin Primer, we're going to dive even deeper into the fascinating world of this cryptocurrency. We'll show you how to buy and stash your Bitcoin safely, explore its potential as an investment, and uncover its real-world applications. So, whether you're new to the crypto scene or a seasoned pro, stick with us as we uncover the secrets of Bitcoin.

Chapter 3:

Bitcoin receiving and storing.

Ahoy there, crypto adventurers! Welcome to the third chapter of your Bitcoin journey. Here, we discuss how you can get your hands on some digital gold. It's a bit like a treasure hunt, but there are few technical maps. So, tighten your bootstraps and get ready to discover the world of buying, storing and protecting your Bitcoin.

Bitcoin Market:

Buying on exchanges, first things first, if you want to join the Bitcoin club you will need to make a purchase. And that's why you want to go to a crypto exchange – think of it as a digital marketplace for cryptocurrencies

Exchanges are like crowded marketplaces where traders buy and sell bitcoins. You can find different cryptocurrencies, not just Bitcoin. It's a bit like a virtual Wall Street, with digital currencies instead of stocks . These platforms match buyers and sellers, making it easy to exchange your hard-earned money for a piece of the Bitcoin pie.

To get started, you'll usually need to sign up, go through some authentication for security purposes (such as proving you're not a robot), and then you're good to go. As with any financial platform, you may want to do your homework and choose a popular variation with a good track record. Safety and ease of use are key.

The Quick Stop,

Bitcoin ATM, If you are more of a manual user, you may want to check out a Bitcoin ATM. They look like regular ATMs, but instead of spitting cash they let you buy and sometimes sell cryptocurrency.

All you need is a digital wallet, some cash or a debit/credit card, and you're good to go. You scan your wallet's QR code at an ATM, insert your cash or card, and the bitcoin appears in your wallet. It's like magic!

Now, keep in mind that Bitcoin ATMs can have higher fees compared to online exchanges, so there is a trade-off between convenience and cost.

Hot or cold:

choose your bitcoin wallet,

With your shiny new bitcoins in hand, you'll want to put them away. Enter the digital wallet, your personal savings account for crypto currencies. We got two types to choose from: hot and cold.

Hot wallets are your everyday wallets, available online for fast access. They come in a variety of flavors – web-based, mobile apps, or desktop apps. They're perfect for small projects and easy access, like your back pocket wallet. However, they are more exposed to online threats, so keep the amount you keep there to a minimum.

But for a cold wallet, it's the Fort Knox of crypto storage. They're offline, which makes them super safe. Hardware wallets, paper wallets and physical tokens also fall into this category. They are like the digital equivalent of burying your treasure chest deep underground. These are the ways you can safely store significant amounts of Bitcoin.

Your wallet will give you a unique address, your public key. It's what you share with others when they want to send you Bitcoin. Your private key, on the other hand, is your private code, which allows you to authorize transactions. Keep it nearby and guard it like your grandmother's secret cookie recipe. You lose your private key, you're locked out of your treasure chest.

Safety and security:

Protecting your digital gold,

Now, let's talk about saving your treasures. You don't want any scallywags stealing your hard-earned bitcoins. Here are a few tips to stay safe:

1. **Back up your wallet:** Always back up your wallet, especially if it's a software wallet. You never know when your computer might crash.

2. **Update software:** Update your wallet software to protect against potential vulnerabilities.

3. **Enable two-factor authentication:** Most exchanges and wallet services offer two-factor authentication. It's like having a second lock on your treasure chest.

4. **Watch out for Phishing:** Watch out for phishing attempts. Hackers will try to impersonate legitimate businesses to steal your keys. Double check the URLs to make sure you are going to the right websites.

5. **Protect your private key:** Protect your private key with your life. It's your digital private handshake.

6. **Consider a hardware wallet:** If you want more Bitcoin, invest in a hardware wallet. They are like unbreakable safes for your cryptocurrency digital gold

The Great Divide:

Fractional Bitcoin Ownership.

Now, you're probably thinking, "I can't accept more Bitcoin!" Well, don't worry, you don't have to. Bitcoin is divisible, and you can have fractions of it. In fact, most people buy small and hold on. You can have as much or as little as you like, and the smallest thing is called satoshi. It's like owning a piece of digital history.

Keeping it safe:

your digital piggy bank

Your bitcoins are valuable, so treat them like gold. Consider diversifying your investments. Just as you wouldn't put all your money in one stock, don't put all your crypto in one basket. Spread the money and look into other cryptocurrencies if you're feeling adventurous.

Bitcoin is a good store of value, but it's always a good idea to have a diversified portfolio. Cryptos are known for their price volatility, so having a stable asset can help balance your investment.

Wrapping it up

That's a wrap for Chapter 3. You've learned how to get your hands on some Bitcoin by researching exchanges and ATMs. You also know how to feel safe and secure in your digital wallet, hot or cold. And remember, you don't have to buy all of a bitcoin; You can purchase a small portion and slowly build your digital fortune.

Chapter 4:

Sending and Receiving Bitcoin.

Ahoy, crypto navigators! In Chapter 4 of your Bitcoin Primer, we're diving into the thrilling world of sending and receiving Bitcoin. It's time to master the art of crypto transactions, like a digital pirate navigating the vast seas of the blockchain. So, hoist the sails and let's set forth on this exciting journey!

Where's Your Treasure Map:

Bitcoin Addresses,

Every crypto adventure starts with a destination. In the world of Bitcoin, that destination is called a Bitcoin address. Think of it as your treasure map, guiding you to your digital riches.

A Bitcoin address is a unique combination of letters and numbers, kind of like a postal address for the digital realm. This is where you want your Bitcoins to go when you're receiving them. You share your address with others when you want them to send you Bitcoins. Just like you wouldn't keep your physical address a secret if you wanted someone to send you a letter, you wouldn't keep your Bitcoin address hidden if you want someone to send you crypto.

But there's a catch – while your Bitcoin address is public and safe to share, it's not your secret code. You also have something called a private key, which is like your secret handshake. It's what you use to authorize transactions, like saying, "Yes, this treasure is mine!"

The Gold Coins:

Sending Bitcoin,

Alright, you've got your map (Bitcoin address) and your key (private key). Now, it's time to send some crypto gold. Just like in the real world, you can send your Bitcoins to another address.

Here's how it works.

1. **Recipient's Address:** First, you need the Bitcoin address of the person you want to send your treasure to. Make sure you've got it right, or your coins could end up in the wrong chest.

2. **Amount:** Decide how much treasure you want to send. You can send fractions of a Bitcoin if you'd like. Just be sure not to send more than you have in your treasure chest.

3. **Fees:** Like crossing a bridge, there's usually a toll. Miners who validate and record transactions expect a small fee for their efforts. The higher the fee, the faster your transaction is likely to be confirmed.

4. **Confirmation:** Once you've filled in all the details, you'll review and confirm the transaction. It's kind of like double-checking your map and making sure you're sending the right treasure to the right place.

5. **Private Key:** Before the transaction is officially sent, you'll need to use your private key to unlock your treasure chest and authorize the transfer.

Once your transaction is out in the sea of the blockchain, miners will scoop it up, validate it, and add it to the ledger. It's like sending a message in a bottle and waiting for someone to find and read it. These miners work tirelessly to ensure everything is in order, and it takes some time, typically around 10 minutes for the first confirmation.

Speed Bumps: Transaction Fees and Confirmation Times

You might be wondering, "Why do I need to pay fees, and why does it take time for confirmations?" Well, let's shed some light on that.

Transaction Fees: Fees are like the toll you pay for crossing a bridge. Miners are the gatekeepers of the blockchain, and they expect a little something for their efforts. The more you're willing to pay, the higher the priority your transaction gets. It's like paying extra for fast shipping – your package (in this case, your transaction) gets there quicker.

Confirmation Times: The blockchain is like a crowded sea, and your transaction is just one of many boats. Miners work through a queue of transactions, and it takes time to validate and record them. The first confirmation takes about 10 minutes, and additional confirmations add extra layers of security. Most merchants and exchanges wait for a few confirmations before accepting your payment, ensuring it's legitimate.

The Digital Wallet:

Your Trusted Ship.

Now, let's talk about your trusty vessel in this crypto sea – your digital wallet. It's your go-to tool for sending and receiving Bitcoin, just like a ship is essential for a sailor. Your wallet stores your private keys, making it easy to manage your treasure.

Remember, you've got two main wallet types to choose from: hot and cold. Hot wallets are connected to the internet and are super handy for everyday transactions. They come in various forms, like web-based wallets, mobile apps, and desktop applications. But remember, they're more vulnerable to online threats, so don't store your entire treasure there.

Cold wallets, on the other hand, are the ironclad ships of the crypto world. They're offline and offer maximum security. Hardware wallets, paper wallets, and physical tokens are some examples. These are your choice for storing significant amounts of Bitcoin, where you need the ultimate protection.

Wrapping It Up

As you sail through the world of Bitcoin, remember that it's not just about making transactions; it's part of a more significant financial revolution. Bitcoin challenges traditional financial systems, putting more power in the hands of everyday people.

Bitcoin:

A lifeline for the unbanked and a digital gold store of value.

Bitcoin is a digital currency that provides a way to access and manage funds in remote locations or countries with unstable financial systems. It is also seen as a store of value, like gold, and can be used to protect against inflation.

In the next chapter, we will discuss the exciting world of Bitcoin as an investment. We'll discuss the history of the Bitcoin price, its volatility, and various investment options.

Chapter 5:

Bitcoin as an investment.

Ahoy, crypto investors! Welcome to Chapter 5 of your Bitcoin Primer. This is where the adventure turns into fun as we delve deeper into Bitcoin as an investment. Get ready to ride the crypto roller coaster, learn about its price history, its volatility, investment strategies, and even take a peek into the crystal ball for some future predictions. It's all hands on deck for this thrilling voyage!

The Crypto Wild West:

Bitcoin Price History,
When it comes to Bitcoin, you've probably heard the term "price volatility" thrown around like confetti at a party. That's because bitcoin's price history has been a wild ride, to say the least.

Humble beginnings: In 2010 you could have an entire bitcoin for less than a dollar – yes, you read that right. Fast forward to December 2017, when one bitcoin was trading around $20,000 per coin. That's a meteoric rise!

The Big Swings: But hold on to your hat, because the roller coaster got a lot of loops. In 2018, Bitcoin took a nose-dive in value, dropping back down to $3,000 by the end of the year. Those skyrocketing prices have many people scratching their heads.

Resilience: Despite its ups and downs, Bitcoin has shown incredible resilience. It has been declared dead more times than we can count, but it always bounces back, stronger than ever.

HODLing and Trading: Financial Investments
There are two main ways to invest Bitcoin in the crypto world: HODLing and trading. Wrap it up in plain English.

HODLing: This is a bit of an inside joke in the crypto community. It comes from the misspelling of "hold," and is all about buying and holding Bitcoin, no matter what the market does. HODLers believe in Bitcoin's long-term potential and are not bothered by short-term price fluctuations. It's like buying a prized painting and storing it in your attic, hoping that one day it will be worth a million dollars.

Business: On the other end of the spectrum, we've got marketing. This is for people who enjoy market entertainment. Traders try to take advantage of short-term price increases, buying low and selling high. It's like buying and selling stocks, but with a dash of crypto magic.

Risk and reward:

It's a roller coaster, remember the roller coaster ride mentioned earlier? Well, that's Bitcoin for you. It is known as a volatile price, which means that it can make big gains, but also big losses.

Rewards: We have seen stories of people who have already invested in Bitcoin and become crypto millionaires. The prospect of high returns is what attracts many people to the crypto world. It's like a treasure hunt; You strike gold.

Risk: But let's not forget that high rewards come with high risk. Bitcoin prices can rise dramatically, and if you are not prepared for it, you could be on the losing end of a roller coaster ride. It's important to only invest what you can afford and do your research.

The Prophecies:

Crystal Ball Watching, Now, let's look at the crypto crystal ball and see what the future holds for Bitcoin. Remember that talking about any future investment is a bit like reading tea leaves. Interesting, but not exactly scientific.

Bullish prediction: Some people think the price of bitcoin will continue to rise. They point to factors such as the rise in institutional investment, increasing adoption, and the scarcity of bitcoins (only 21 million will be in circulation). You seem to believe that your treasure map leads you to a chest full of gold.

Bearish predictions: On the flip side, there are those who believe the price of bitcoin is in a bubble that will eventually burst. Concerns over legal challenges, environmental issues (bitcoin mining consumes electricity), and possible competition from other cryptocurrencies are raised as if they doubt the existence of treasure maps.

Middle: Of course there are some who believe the future is somewhere in between. Bitcoin is believed to have ups and downs, like a roller coaster of highs and lows.

Bitcoin and your portfolio:

Bitcoin is a high-risk, high-reward asset. It is a tour of the world of investing. So it's a good idea to balance your investments. Don't put all your coins into one chest; spread them out among various assets.

Like a well-diversified portfolio in the stock market, consider having an asset mix that could include stocks, bonds, real estate, and yes, a portion of your portfolio in bitcoin. This diversification helps cushion the effect of what bitcoins fluctuating value can have on your total wealth.

Wrapping It Up

And there you have it, your guide to the exciting world of bitcoin as an investment. We studied its roller coaster price history, HODLing and trading strategies, and looked into the crypto crystal ball to predict the future.

In the next chapter, we will enter the realm of using bitcoin for payments. We explore how to use bitcoin to pay for goods and services, hire merchants, and even use bitcoin for money transfers. So, get ready for another adventure in the world of crypto-payments!

Chapter 6:

Bitcoin used for payments.

Ahoy there, crypto spenders! Chapter 6 of your Bitcoin Primer is all about using Bitcoin for payments. It's like having a wallet full of digital gold coins ready to be spent. We'll explore how Bitcoin can be used to purchase goods and services, look at merchant adoption, and delve into the world of using Bitcoin to settle remittances So, grab your digital wallet, and let's embark on this exciting journey in the world of crypto payments!

Bitcoin's shopping spree:

Payment for goods and services, You may have heard that Bitcoin is the future of currency, but what does that mean for everyday spending? Well, that means you can pay for more things with it, just like you do with your regular cash.

Online merchants: Many online stores now accept Bitcoin as an alternative form of payment. It's as simple as choosing bitcoin as your payment method and scanning a QR code with your digital wallet. It's like using a virtual credit card.

Physical stores: While this is not as common as cash or card payments, some brick and mortar stores accept Bitcoin as well. You will need a smartphone and a Bitcoin wallet app for these services. Imagine waving your digital magic wand in return.

Gift Cards: Some platforms allow you to buy gift cards with Bitcoin, which you can then use at retail outlets. It's a bit like exchanging your treasure for a universal gift card.

Travel and accommodation: You can use Bitcoin to book flights, hotels, and more. It's like paying for a vacation with a piece of digital heaven.

Food Delivery: Hungry for pizza? Some food delivery services allow you to pay with Bitcoin. It's like ordering a party with a little digital spice.

Charitable donations: Many non-profit organizations accept bitcoin donations. It's a way to give back and do good in the world.

Speed and cost:

Bitcoin transactions have their own advantages and disadvantages compared to traditional payment methods. Let's break it down:

Speed: Bitcoin transactions can be lightning fast. You can send money anywhere in the world in minutes, which is especially convenient for international payments. Traditional bank transfers, on the other hand, can take days, and transferring money across borders can feel like forever.

Price: Bitcoin transactions can be cheap, especially for international transactions. Traditional banks and payment processors typically charge high fees for cross-border transactions, while bitcoin fees are often a fraction of that. It's like choosing between an expensive plane ticket and a cheap flight.

Volatility: But here's the catch – Bitcoin prices can be volatile. This means that if you hold your Bitcoin for too long before spending it, its value can change dramatically. Therefore, it is important to consider this when paying.

Merchant Recruitment:

The fancy word for how many businesses and stores accept Bitcoin is merchant approval. The good news is that it has slowly increased over the years. Big companies like Microsoft, Overstock, and AT&T embrace bitcoin, and there are thousands of small businesses that have also jumped on the crypto wagon.

Online merchants: You can buy electronics, clothes, and even book your next flight with Bitcoin on platforms like Newegg, Bitrefill, and CheapAir.

Travel and Accommodation: When planning a trip, consider using Bitcoin to book flights and hotels through websites like Expedia and TravelbyBit.

Food and Drink: Hungry? Some restaurants and cafes accept bitcoin payment. It's like enjoying a meal sprinkled with digital flavors.

Gift Cards: If you're looking for gift cards for your favorite causes, check out services like BitPay and eGifter.

Charities: Don't forget to give back – you can donate in bitcoin to organizations like the Red Cross and Save the Children.

Sending money home:

Sending money to friends or family across borders can be expensive and time-consuming. That's where bitcoin can be a game changer, especially for remittances. People working abroad can send money home at a fraction of the cost compared to traditional methods. Bitcoin's speed and low cost make it a practical choice for international shipments.

Here is how it works. You may already have enough Bitcoin or go purchase some at a cryptocurrency exchange, then send Bitcoin to you friend or family. They take the Bitcoin and exchange it for their local currency. It's like shipping a digital care plan.

Cost savings: With no high fees or intermediaries, Bitcoin can save you a significant amount of shipping costs.

Speed: International bank transfers can take days, but bitcoin transfers are usually completed in minutes.

Word of caution: Fluctuating prices

While Bitcoin offers a wide range of benefits, it's important to be aware of how prices can fluctuate. Bitcoin prices can fluctuate dramatically, which means that the amount you pay for a good or service with Bitcoin today may be different tomorrow. It is like shopping in a store where prices keep changing.

Wrapping It Up

That concludes Chapter 6, where you learned how to use Bitcoin to pay bills, shop online, eat out and book flights, and send money internationally. You now have the tools to navigate the world of crypto-payments like a skilled sailor.

In the next chapter, we examine how bitcoin compares to traditional currencies. We'll take a closer look at the differences between centralized and embedded currencies, compare bitcoin to fiat currencies and gold, and go over the benefits of this brave new world of finance. So, get ready for another exciting step in your crypto journey!

Chapter 7:

Bitcoin VS Traditional Currencies.

Oh, fellow crypto researchers! In Chapter 7 of your Bitcoin Primer, we're going to start an interesting journey with a comparison between Bitcoin and traditional currencies. It's like sailing with the legendary pirates of old, only our treasure is digital and our ship is blockchain. We'll break down the differences between centralized and decentralized currencies, compare bitcoin to fiat currencies and gold, and demonstrate the enormous benefits of this brave new world of finance. So, let's raise the anchor and sail into the crypto sea!

Talk of two currencies:

Centralized and decentralized. Imagine that the financial world is a vast ocean, and money is the only boat that sails in it. In this ocean, we have two distinct currencies: centralized and decentralized.

Static currencies: These are traditional currencies that you are already familiar with, such as dollars, euros, or yen. It is issued and administered by a central government, usually the government and its central bank. Imagine a fleet of large cargo ships where captains and crew control the rudder, and determine the course of the ship.

Decentralized currencies: This is where Bitcoin enters the scene. It's like a pirate ship in a sea of crypto, operating independently of any central authority. Instead, it relies on a decentralized network of trusted users and record transactions on a public ledger called the blockchain. There is no commander or special authority; It's like a team of digital sailors working together.

The struggle for power

Decentralized currencies give greater power to the governments and central banks that issue and manage them. They can decide on supply, interest rates, and even print more money. The king seems to be able to make more money whenever he wants.

In other words, Bitcoin and decentralized currencies are taking that power away from centralized control and putting it in the hands of the people. The rules are codified in law, and change requires consensus among network participants. It is like a group of sailors agreeing on the course of their ship.

Gold has long been considered a treasure trove. It is a precious metal that has been used as currency for centuries. Bitcoin is often hailed as "digital gold." So how does it compare?

Rarity: Both gold and bitcoin are limited resources. Only a certain amount of each is available. Gold is mined from the earth, while Bitcoin has a record 21 million coins. This scarcity is a key factor in their value.

Portability: Gold is not an easy commodity to carry around. It is heavy and can be difficult to transport. However, Bitcoin is as small as the digital part. You can remember it on your smartphone, hardware wallet, or even your private key, and it's with you wherever you go.

Divisible: Gold is not easily divisible. You cannot withdraw a fraction of your gold for a small purchase. However, Bitcoin is highly divisible. You can get all of the bitcoin or a fraction known as satoshi.

Digital Nature: Perhaps the most important difference is that Bitcoin is purely digital. It exists in the digital realm, whereas gold is a physical asset. It's like comparing a treasure chest buried deep in the sand to a treasure map stored in a digital vault.

Bitcoin vs. Bitcoin Gold:

World advantage of Bitcoin. Now that we've compared bitcoin to traditional currencies and gold, let's dive into the benefits of this brave new world of finance.

Accessibility: Bitcoin is like a financial lifeline for those without traditional banking services. Bitcoin provides a way to access and manage funds in remote locations or countries with unstable financial systems. It is like a bridge connecting the unbanked with the global economy.

Secure: The blockchain technology underpinning bitcoin is highly secure. Once a transaction is recorded on the blockchain, it is nearly impossible to change it. This level of protection exceeds that of many traditional financial systems.

Transparency: Each bitcoin transaction is recorded on a public ledger, providing transparency and traceability. This is in stark contrast to traditional banking, where transactions can be private and sometimes hidden.

Ownership: Bitcoin gives you complete control and access to your money. There are no middlemen, and you can send and receive bitcoins without the need for a third party. It's like owning your ship and taking it wherever you want.

Financial Inclusion: Bitcoin is a lifeline for those without traditional banking services. Bitcoin provides a way to access and manage funds in remote locations or countries with unstable financial systems.

Inflation protection: As governments print more currency, inflation can cause traditional currencies to depreciate. Bitcoin, with its scarcity and deflationary nature, provides a hedge from inflation.

Risks and uncertainty: Of course, any great journey comes with its share of risks and challenges. Bitcoin is not unbreakable:

Regulatory status: Governments around the world are still trying to figure out how to regulate bitcoin. Some have embraced it, others have strictly regulated it or even banned it. It's like sailing through a sea of rules and regulations.

Illegitimacy: Bitcoin has been associated with illegal activities, mainly due to its pseudonymity. While not inherently illegal, it has been used for things like money laundering and dark web purchases. It looks like a pirate ship that hasn't always been used for noble purposes.

Security Vulnerabilities: While the blockchain itself is secure, the infrastructure around it, such as exchanges and wallets, can be vulnerable to security breaches such as hacking etc. It's like protecting your ship from pirates on the high seas.

Wrapping It Up

As we wrap up Chapter 7, remember that comparing Bitcoin to traditional currencies is like an exciting journey through the crypto seas. While Bitcoin offers incredible returns, it's important to be aware of the risks and uncertainties that surround it.

In the next chapter, we will dive into the heart of blockchain technology and innovation. We will explore how blockchain works, learn about smart contracts and second-tier solutions, and unlock new features beyond just payments. So, get ready for another exciting journey in the world of crypto technology!

Chapter 8:

Blockchain Technology and Innovation.

Ahoy, crypto tech enthusiasts! In Chapter 8 of your Bitcoin Primer, we're about to embark on an exciting journey through the heart of blockchain technology and innovation. It's like sailing on a pirate ship, but instead of searching for hidden treasure, we're unlocking the mysteries of the blockchain We'll demystify how blockchain works, explore smart contracts and secondary solutions, and we have discovered a wide world of innovation that goes far beyond just digital gold. So, let's grab a compass and dive into crypto-technology waters!

The Blockchain has been revealed

Imagine a blockchain as a giant ledger that records every bitcoin transaction. But unlike your typical ledger its digital, decentralized and immutable.

Decentralization: Instead of one company, the ledger is managed by thousands of computers around the world. They have a shared map with every sailor on the high seas that marks their voyage.

Transparency: Every transaction is recorded for all to see. You can think of it as a transparent mirror through which you can see any body of water in the ocean.

Immutability: Once something is written on the blockchain, it is there forever. It's like having your name engraved on a treasure chest with no erasure.

Security: Blockchain is virtually hack-proof. Transactions are verified and secured through robust accounting systems. It's like building an impregnable castle to protect your treasure.

Smart contracts: Digital promise keepers

Smart contracts are like the magic of the crypto world. They are self-serving contracts in which the terms of the contract between the buyer and the seller are codified directly in legal terms.

To illustrate:

Imagine that you want to bet on a sporting event. A smart deal can be made that will automatically transfer the winnings to the winner as soon as the results of the game are published. There is no need for mediation; It's like a magic judge.

Applications: Smart contracts can be used for a wide variety of purposes, from insurance payments to supply chains. They are like having a digital genie that makes your wishes work.

Pros: Efficient, transparent, and most importantly, unreliable. This means you don't have to rely on a third party; You can trust the law. It's like a sealed promise of unbreakable magic.

Challenges: However, it is not without its challenges. Flaws in the code can lead to unintended consequences and, in some cases, legal and ethical problems. It's like trying to control an evil spell.

Second solution:

Bitcoin, while secure and transparent, can be a bit slow. Configure a second layer solution, such as Lightning Network. It's like attaching a turbocharger to your ship.

How it works: Instead of recording every transaction on the main blockchain, Lightning Network processes payments. It's like having a secret line of communication between ships in a fleet.

Speed: Electronic Internet connections are almost instantaneous. It's like paying money and the treasure chest looks instantly open.

Scalability: Bitcoin scale helps handle more transactions without hindering the main blockchain. It's like increasing your ship's cargo capacity without increasing it.

Challenges: But it's not without its challenges. Capacity is still evolving, and there are concerns about infrastructure and privacy. It's like upgrading the turbocharger on your ship.

Beyond payments:

While Bitcoin was primarily created to be a digital currency, blockchain technology has expanded to a vast realm of possibilities.

Digital Identity: Blockchain can be used for secure and tamper-proof digital identity authentication. It's like a passport to the digital world.

Election system: Some states are exploring blockchain for a secure and transparent electoral system. They seem to ensure fair elections with unspendable funds.

Supply Chain Management: The main characteristic of blockchain is a transparent and immutable record of all transactions in the supply chain. This makes it easier to trace transactions from source to destination, improves accountability and reduces the risk of fraud

Healthcare: Blockchain is used to manage health records, clinical trials, patient tracking, and improve security, efficiency and transparency. Manages financial reporting in hospitals and reduces data turnaround time and costs

Tokenization of Assets: Real estate, art and stocks can all be tokenized on the blockchain, making ownership traceable. It's like dividing your money into smaller, more manageable units.

Decentralized Finance (DeFi): DeFi platforms allow you to earn interest, borrow, and trade assets without traditional banks. It's like creating a decentralized financial kingdom.

Non-Fungible Tokens (NFTs): NFTs are like digital certificates of authenticity, making unique digital and physical items tradeable. It's like owning a piece of art that no one can counterfeit.

Gaming: Blockchain is also changing the world of gaming by providing unique assets in gaming that players can buy, sell and trade. It's like having digital collectibles in your favorite game.

Challenges in the digital world

Of course, the digital world is not without its challenges.

Scalability: As more applications use blockchain, scalability becomes a major concern. It's like trying to navigate a fleet through a narrow channel.

Laws: Governments are still figuring out how to structure this new world, and laws can vary greatly from place to place. It's like sailing through an ocean filled with ever-changing currents.

Security: While the blockchain itself is secure, the platform and applications built on it can have vulnerabilities. It's like protecting a treasure chest with strange locks.

Wrapping It Up

As we wrap up Chapter 8, it's clear that blockchain technology has immense potential, though the possibilities are still unfolding. We've covered innovative concepts like smart contracts and scaling solutions, but there is still so much unknown territory to explore.

However, with any transformative technology, there are always risks and challenges to consider. In the next chapter, we will take a pragmatic look at some of the issues facing Bitcoin specifically. We'll examine concerns around regulation, illicit usage, and security vulnerabilities.

The goal is to provide a balanced perspective on blockchain, avoiding hype or oversimplification. This technology may facilitate many positive changes, but it's not a panacea. There are still hurdles to overcome before blockchain can be safely integrated into mainstream finance and business.

As we navigate the opportunities and risks of this new world, the goal is to equip you with the knowledge needed to make informed decisions. The seas of crypto investing can certainly be choppy, so developing critical thinking is key. There are no easy answers, despite what overzealous advocates on either side may claim.

The future may be unpredictable, but with patient study we can chart a reasoned course. Look forward to exploring this rapidly changing landscape in the coming chapters. Exciting innovations await, if we steer clear of dangerous waters.

Chapter 9:

The Risks and Challenges of Bitcoin.

Ahoy, brave crypto sailors! In Chapter 9 of your Bitcoin Primer, we guide you straight into choppy waters with risks and challenges that every crypto adventurer should be aware of. It's like sailing through treacherous seas, but with the right knowledge and strategy, you can weather the storm. We will delve into the legal environment and government uncertainties, explore the sometimes murky waters of illegal use, and raise the flag of security vulnerabilities. So, fasten your seatbelts, and let's ride through the crypto storm!

The regulation of murky water

One of the biggest challenges with bitcoin is regulation. Governments around the world are still trying to figure out how to classify and regulate cryptocurrencies. It is like sailing through a sea of water and waves.

Methods: Each country has a different method. Some have embraced cryptocurrency, while others have strictly regulated or banned it. Communities seem to enter their own rules and customs.

Compliance: For cryptocurrency businesses and individuals, keeping up with the ever-changing regulations can be a real challenge. It's like trying to follow a changing map.

Taxation: Cryptocurrency taxation is another complicated issue. In some countries, crypto gains are considered capital gains, while others may classify them as income. It's like dealing with a tax code written in a foreign language.

Dark web and illegal activities

While Bitcoin offers a world of possibilities, it is not without its dark side. It looks like a ship that can be used for both noble and nefarious purposes.

Dark web: Bitcoin is associated with the dark web, where illegal goods and services are often bought and sold. It looks like a ship sometimes used by pirates.

Money laundering: Cryptocurrencies can be used for money laundering due to fake names. It's like trying to hide the origin of your treasure.

Ransomware: Bitcoin has been used by criminals in ransomware attacks, demanding payment in crypto to unlock stolen computers. It's like pirates are taking your data hostage.

Legislative Response: Governments have been increasingly interested in combating these illegal uses, and have enacted stringent regulations in some areas. Pirates are like surfers on the rough seas.

Security Flaw: Protecting your treasure

The world of cryptocurrency can be a treasure trove for hackers. It's like swimming in a tub full of Cyber pirates.

Exchanges and wallets: While the blockchain itself is secure, the platform and applications built on it can have vulnerabilities. Exchanges and wallets are prime targets for hackers. It's like protecting a treasure chest with strange locks.

Phishing: Fraudsters often use phishing emails and websites to trick users into revealing their private keys and credentials. It's like pirates trapping unsuspecting sailors.

Scams: The crypto world has seen its fair share of scams, from Ponzi schemes to fake initial coin offerings (ICOs). It's like meeting shady characters who try to sell you fake maps for hidden treasure.

Best Practices: Following best practices is essential to protecting your treasures. Use a hardware wallet, provide two-factor authentication, and watch out for unsolicited items. It's like fortifying your ship against a pirate attack.

Crypto Answer:

The crypto community doesn't just sit idly by; They are working hard to address these challenges:

Self-regulation: Some in the crypto space are advocating for self-regulation and best practices to keep the industry from shrinking. It is like a group of sailors working together to protect their ships.

Education: Educating users about the risks and how to stay safe with the cryptocurrency is very important. It's like teaching sailors how to navigate treacherous waters.

Innovation: Continuous innovation in blockchain technology provides solutions to many of these challenges. You seem to have discovered new navigation tools to make sailing safer.

Wrapping It Up

As we conclude Chapter 9, it's important to remember that navigating a crypto storm is possible with the right knowledge and preparation. From varying regulations to the illegal use of sometimes murky waters and the need to protect your treasures, being a crypto sailor has the responsibility of understanding these fundamentals.

In the final chapter, we will look into the crystal ball and explore the future of bitcoin and cryptocurrencies. We will consider broader adoption, competition from new digital banks, and forecasts for innovation and growth. So, raise your sails, and let's go to the crypto horizon!

Chapter 10:

Future of Bitcoin and Cryptocurrencies.

Ahoy, fellow crypto adventurers! In our final chapter of the Bitcoin Primer, we're going to gaze into the crystal ball and explore the uncharted waters of the future of Bitcoin and cryptocurrencies. It's like we're setting sail on an epic journey towards the crypto horizon. We'll ponder the possibilities of wider adoption, consider the competition from other digital treasures, and make predictions for the waves of innovation and growth. So, batten down the hatches, and let's set sail towards the crypto horizon!

Wider Adoption:

From Niche to Mainstream. Bitcoin and cryptocurrencies have come a long way from their humble beginnings. It's like witnessing a small fishing village grow into a bustling port city.

Retail Acceptance: As more businesses and retailers accept cryptocurrencies as a form of payment, using Bitcoin for everyday transactions is becoming increasingly common. It's like being able to pay for your groceries with pieces of eight.

Financial Services: Traditional financial institutions are slowly integrating cryptocurrencies into their services. Banks are offering custody solutions, and investment firms are creating cryptocurrency-focused products. It's like having the old-guard institutions recognizing the value of digital gold.

Global Remittances: Bitcoin is making cross-border money transfers more accessible and affordable. It's like sending a message in a bottle that gets delivered instantly.

Emerging Markets: In regions with unstable currencies or limited access to banking services, Bitcoin is a lifeline. It's like offering a lifeboat to those stranded on a desert island.

Financial Inclusion: The unbanked and underbanked populations now have a way to access and manage their finances. It's like providing a treasure map to those who were lost at sea.

The Rising Competition

In the vast crypto seas, Bitcoin has faced competition from a slew of other digital treasures. It's like encountering rival pirate ships vying for the same booty.

Altcoins: There are thousands of alternative cryptocurrencies, each with its unique features and purposes. Ethereum, for instance, is like a ship with an entire fleet of smaller boats, each serving a different function.

Smart Contracts: Smart contract platforms like Ethereum have carved their own niche, offering features and capabilities that Bitcoin doesn't possess. It's like having a rival pirate crew with their own special skills.

Stablecoins: Stablecoins, like USDC and USDT, offer the stability of fiat currencies while still operating on blockchain technology. They're like treasure chests that never lose their value.

Central Bank Digital Currencies (CBDCs): Some governments are exploring the idea of creating their digital currencies, which could rival cryptocurrencies. It's like a new fleet of government-issued ships entering the crypto seas.

Predictions for Innovation and Growth

The crypto world is constantly evolving, and predicting its future is like forecasting the weather on the high seas – full of uncertainty, but with patterns that can guide us.

Scalability Solutions: As cryptocurrencies gain wider adoption, the need for scalability solutions becomes even more pressing. It's like upgrading your ship to handle a larger cargo.

Regulatory Clarity: Governments will likely continue to develop and refine their cryptocurrency regulations, providing more clarity for businesses and users. It's like creating standardized navigation charts for all sailors.

Security Enhancements: With the increasing value and usage of cryptocurrencies, security will become an even more critical focus. It's like fortifying your ship to withstand any storm.

NFT Evolution: Non-fungible tokens (NFTs) will likely continue to evolve and find applications beyond digital art and collectibles. It's like discovering new treasures hidden deep in the ocean.

DeFi Expansion: Decentralized finance (DeFi) is poised for significant growth, offering more financial services and products to users. It's like building a bustling port city in the crypto world.

Mass Adoption: Bitcoin and cryptocurrencies could become as common as using credit cards or cash today. It's like witnessing the transformation of the entire financial landscape.

Wrapping It Up

As we conclude our Bitcoin Primer, remember that the world of cryptocurrencies is still in its early stages. It's a bit like being a sailor in the Age of Exploration, with vast uncharted waters ahead.

So, set your course, prepare your crew, and get ready for the next great crypto adventure. Whether you're new to this world or a seasoned crypto sailor, the horizon is waiting, and the future is yours to explore. As they say in the crypto seas, "Hodl on and may your sails be ever filled with favorable winds!"